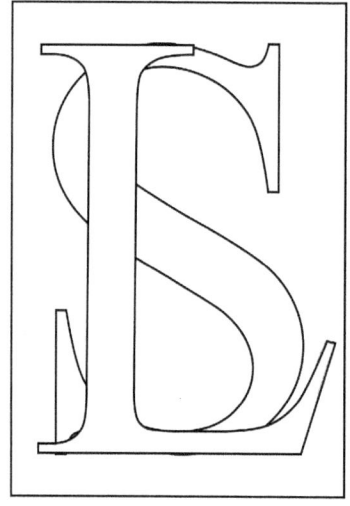

+ SKYLER LOYD +

~

For my Mother,
She is the strongest woman I know.
I hope to make her proud.

+And for my Grandmother,
She inspired me so much, I miss her deeply.

Both of these women were there for me. And I don't know where I'd be without them.

~

+ INTRO +

~

The Earth Opened Wide: The Complete Artwork Collection From the 2020 acclaimed musical album.

Originally released on August 11th 2020 "The Earth Opened Wide" by Skyler Loyd is an Abstract, New Age / Experimental Musical work. Along with it, Loyd created multiple Abstract art pieces that go with the album. The art pieces weren't shared as much as the album was, but the art pieces played a major and critical part in the creation of the musical album.

This book shows every art piece Skyler Loyd created to help give the album a body and soul. And to help give the album a more visual point of view.
This book includes alternate versions of artwork as well as never-before seen art pieces. This book is like a mini art gallery.

I truly hope you enjoy!

~

+ S K Y L E R L O Y D +

THE EARTH OPENED WIDE

THE COMPLETE ARTWORK COLLECTION FROM THE 2020 ACCLAIMED MUSICAL ALBUM

THE DOORWAY //

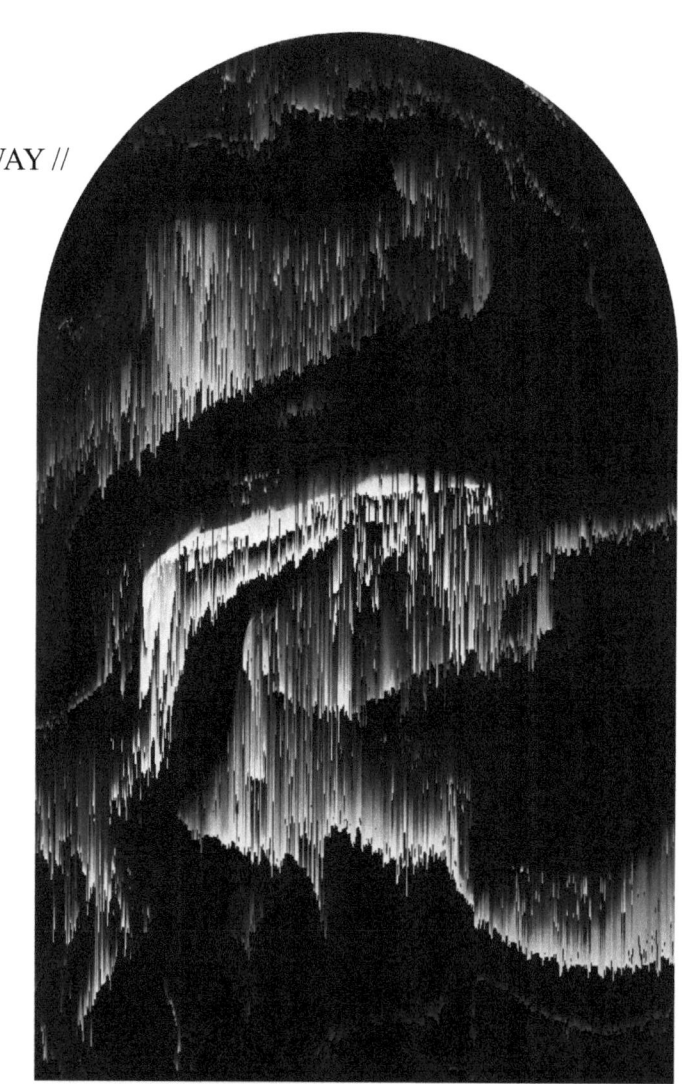

There is both beauty and pain to be seen in this collection.
"The Doorway" was one of the first pieces to be created during the writing process for the album. Representing new beginnings and the act of leaving the old way behind.
A mix of Oil on Canvas clashed with Digital Rendering.

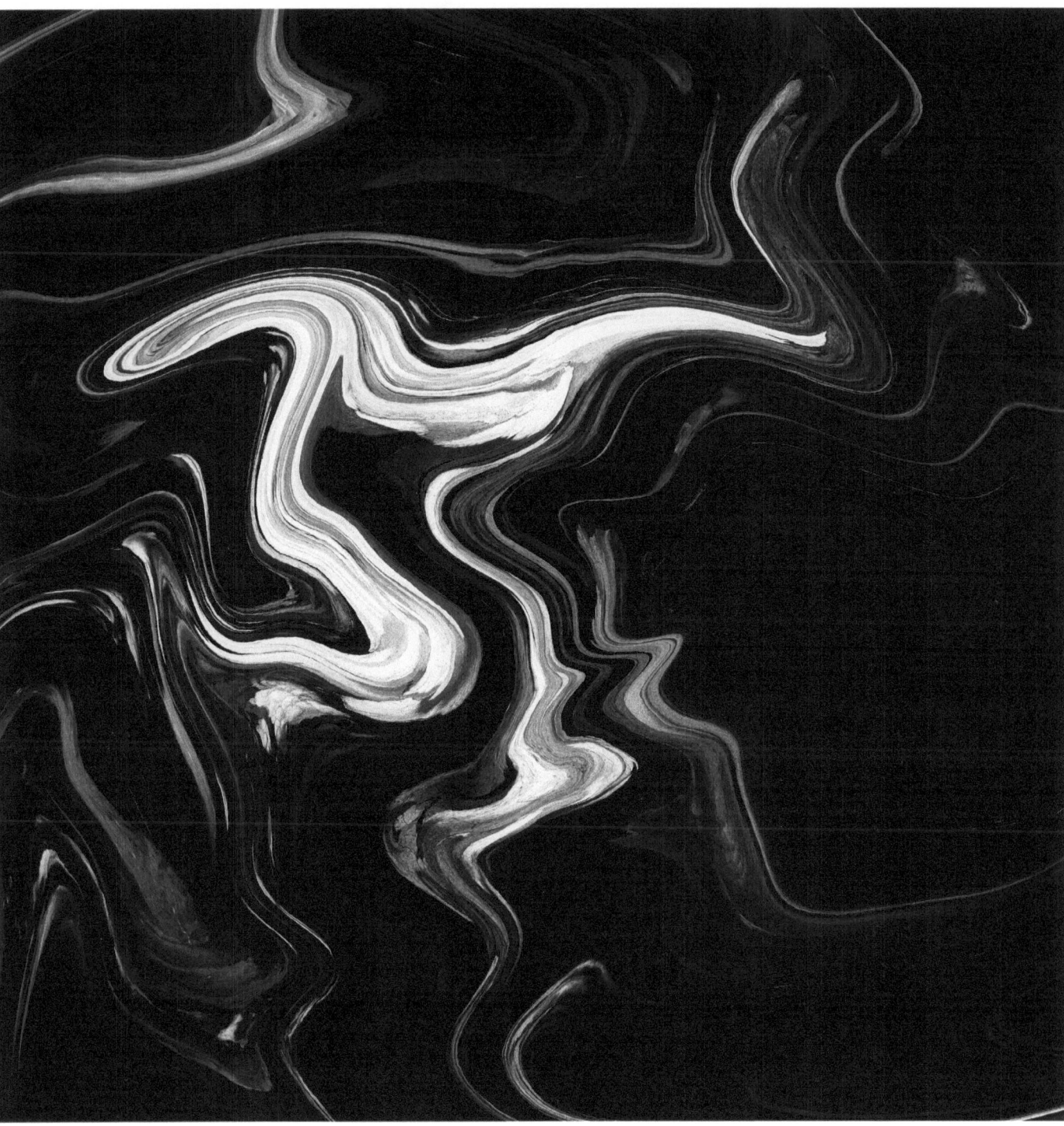

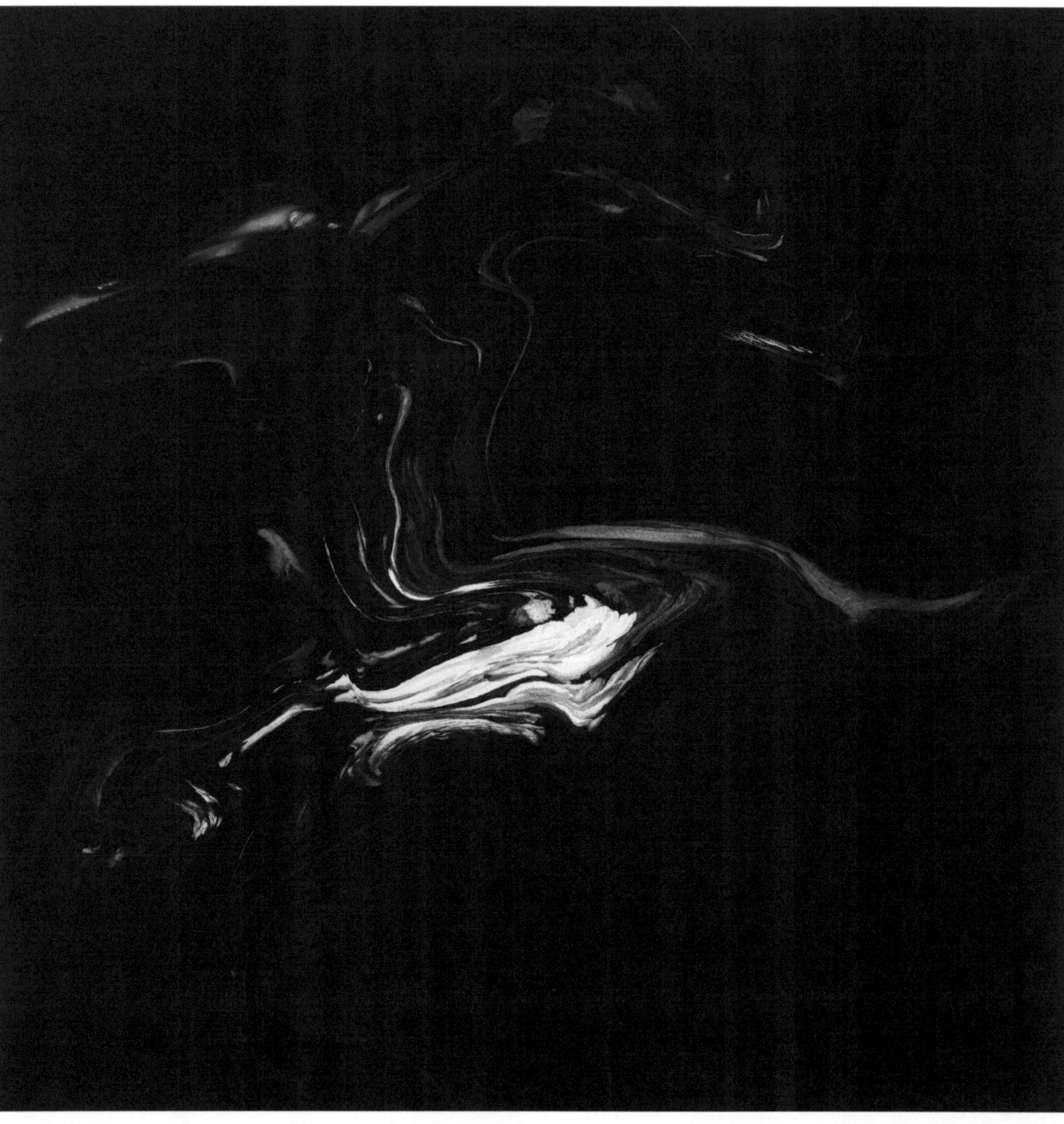

~

The overall color palette for the album is very dark. I wanted it to match how I was feeling in the moment. During the making of this album I was going through some of the
Hardest times of my life. I was diagnosed with Clinical Depression and Anxiety. I was seeking treatment at the time I started on these pieces and writing music.
I can not stress how important mental health is; depression is real and so is anxiety. And reaching out was one of the hardest things I ever did.
But I couldn't hide how I was feeling anymore. I felt as if I was dying. All this artwork and music on the album was influenced by my Depression.
But since the release of the album, I feel like I've grown as a human. My soul feels alive more than ever. If it wasn't for my family and the artistic outlets I was blessed with I may not have made it to Christmas (2020).

~

+ THE ALBUM COVER +

This is the official album cover for the album. Compared to the rest of the artwork created for this album, this one can seem a bit on the more 'minimal' side. I have an on going theme with all my album covers. I have yet to show my face entirely on them.

But this piece encompasses the feeling of not being in control. Not having control of your emotions and losing your grip on time. When I was at the climax of my depression, I lost all sense of time. I had episodes of confusion when I would sleep for a day at a time.

I felt this piece truly matched the overall story the album told. It was human and yet still had some abstract form. It still encompassed the cataclysmic storm of emotions the album held.

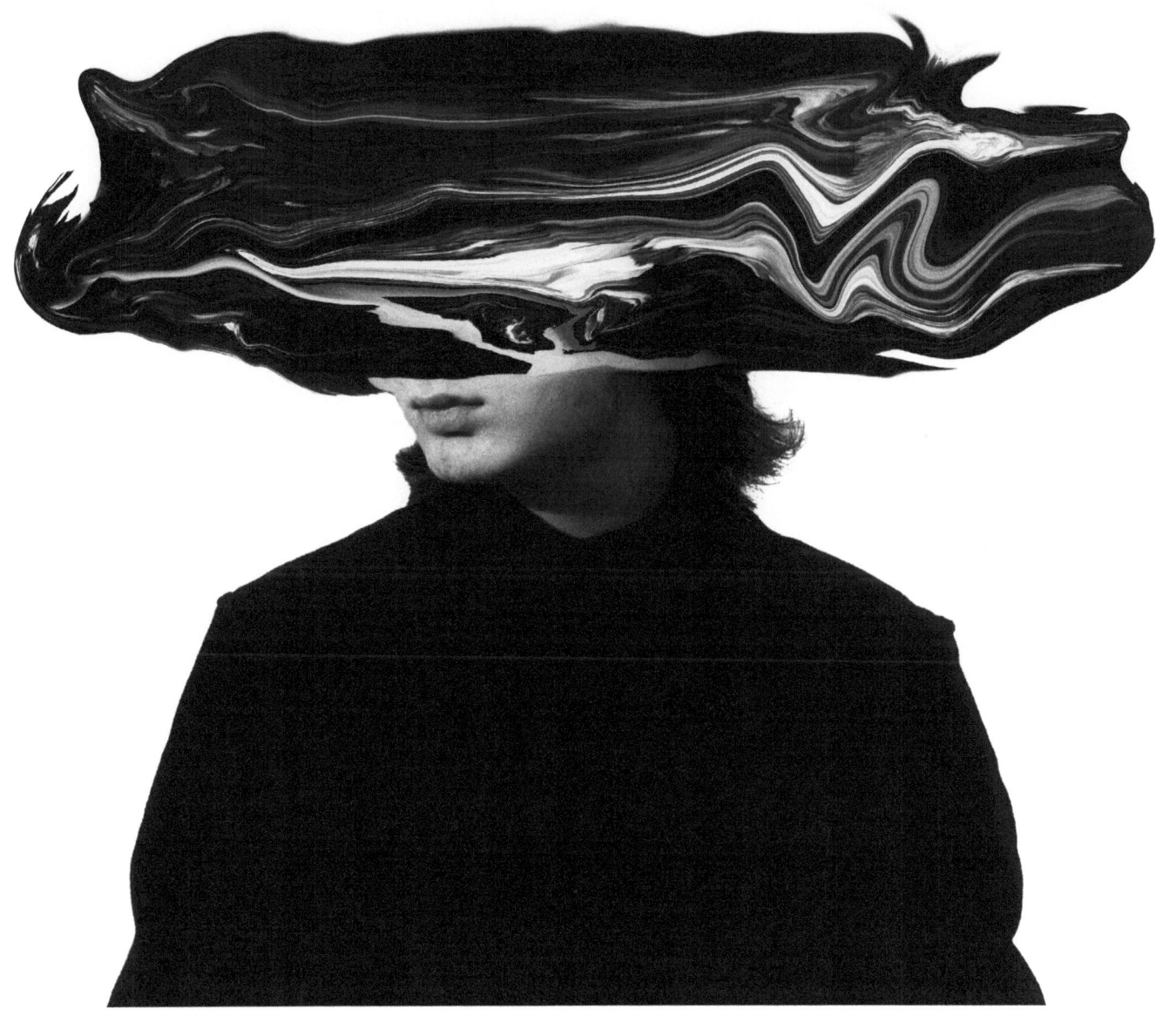

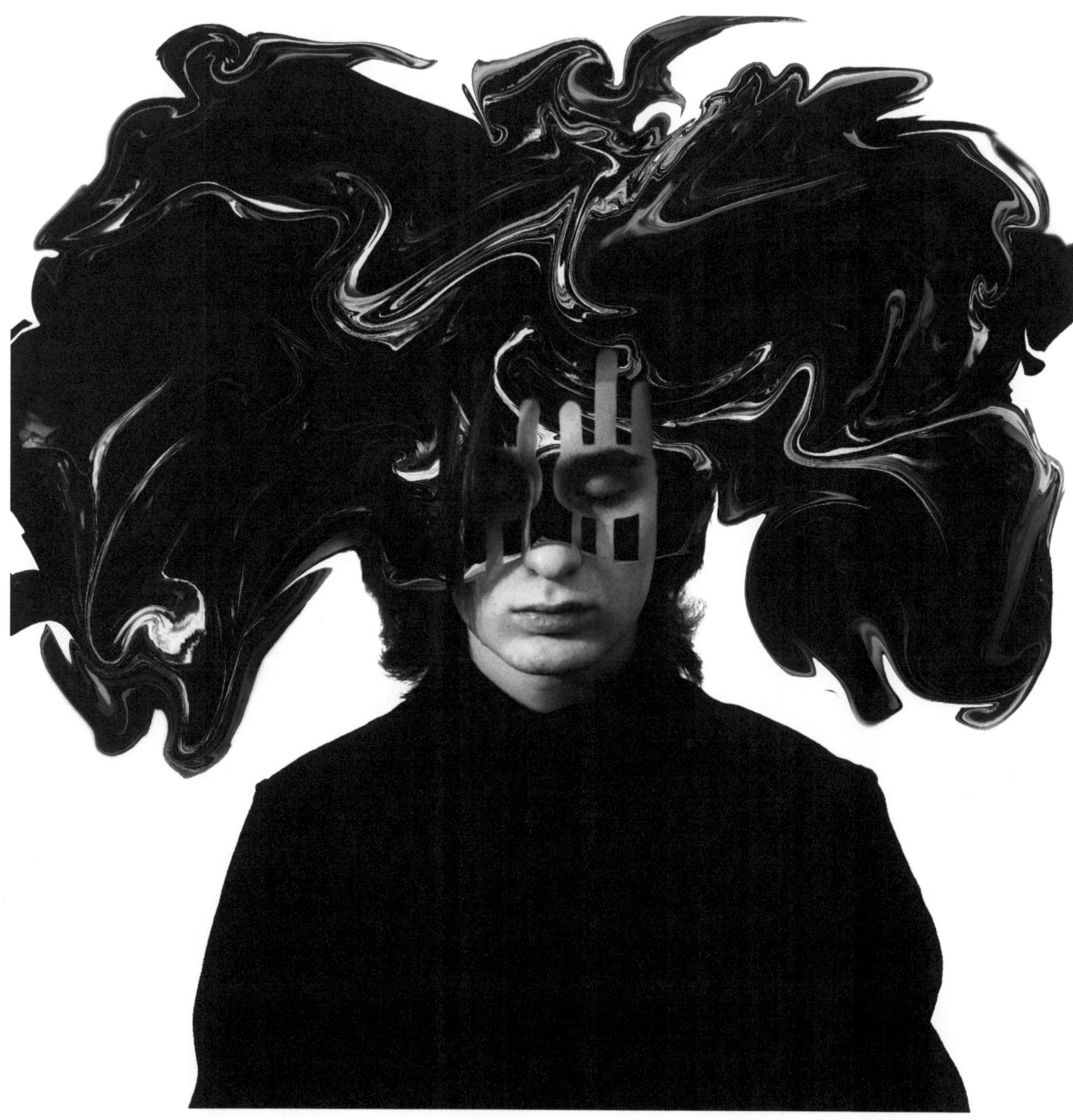

~

The artwork for the album did have some inspiration behind it. This image was inspired by John Everett Millais's "Ophelia"
I found his piece very striking. I was pulled to it and something in me resonated with it. Sometimes I do feel like I'm in cold water. Being pulled underneath. The 1st track on the album is titled "Underwater" and this piece was created to represent it.

Out of all the artwork, this one has the most attention. It's also one of my personal favorites as well.

An alternate version of this piece exists as well.
The same can be said for most all of these art pieces.

~

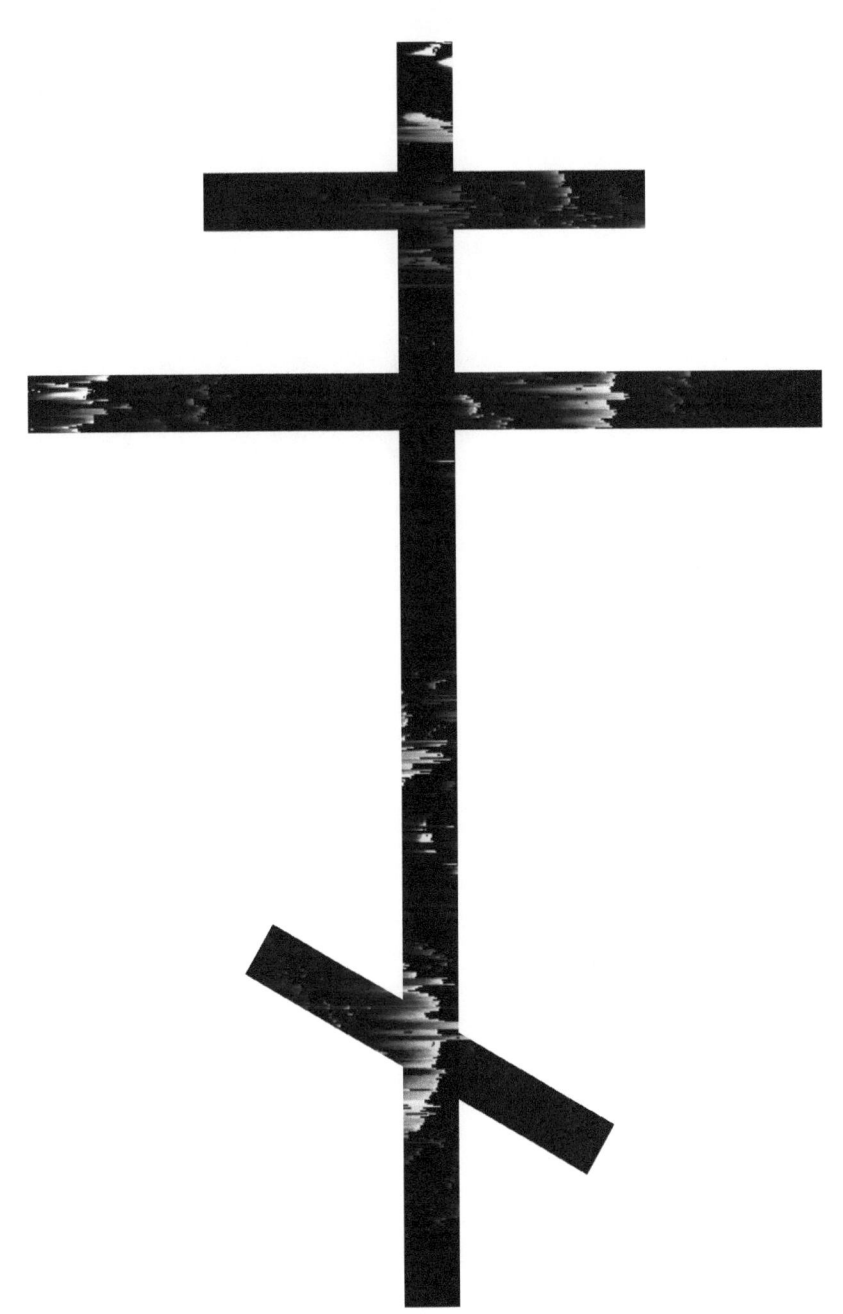

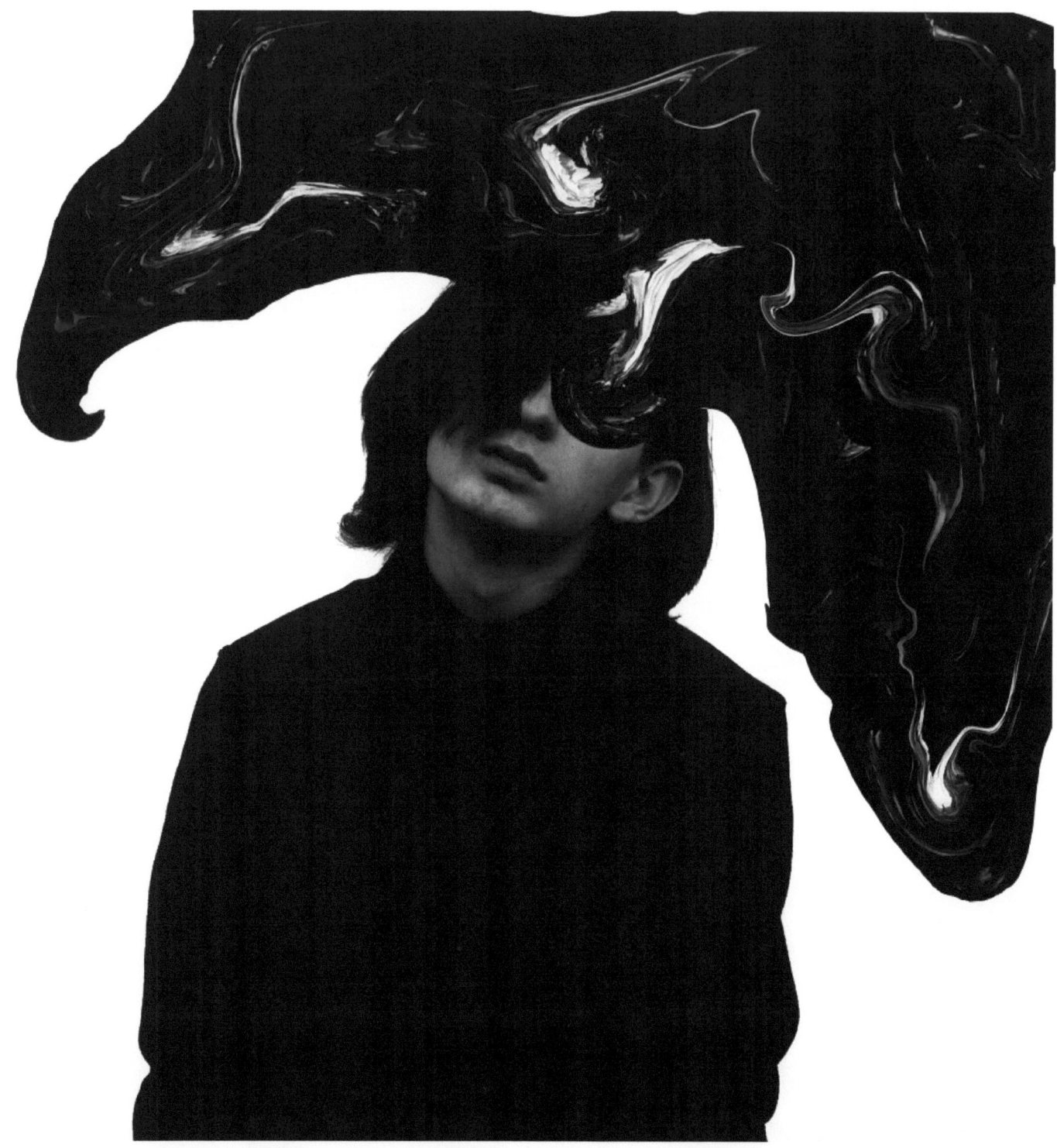

I am very proud of all the artwork that was created for this album. Not just the music, but the artwork represented a staple in not only my life, but in my career. This album means so much to me, and I am truly so happy that it was so well received. As an artist I want to make it my mission to make art that people can feel and talk about.
I hope that someday I can help people through my work.

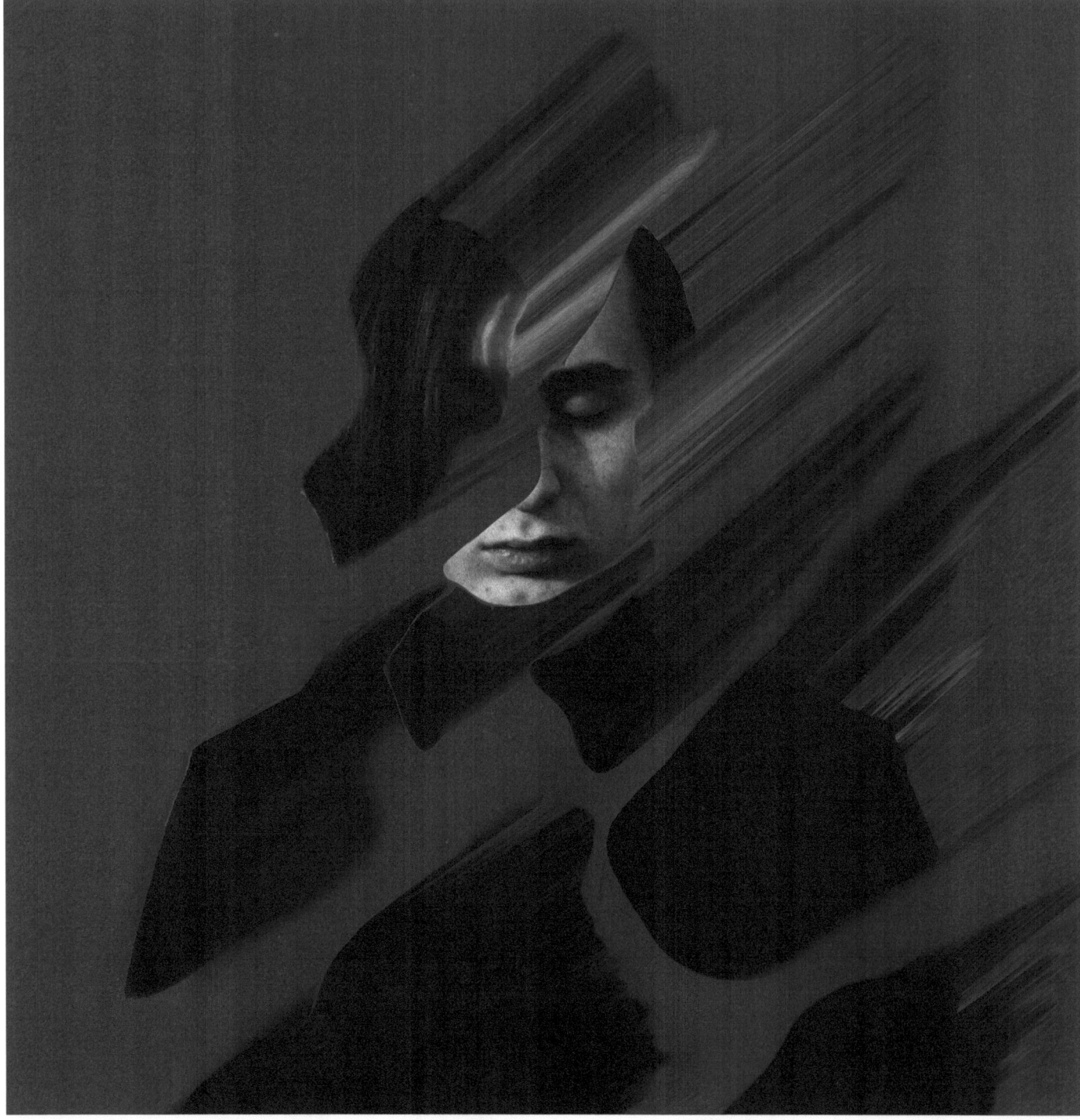

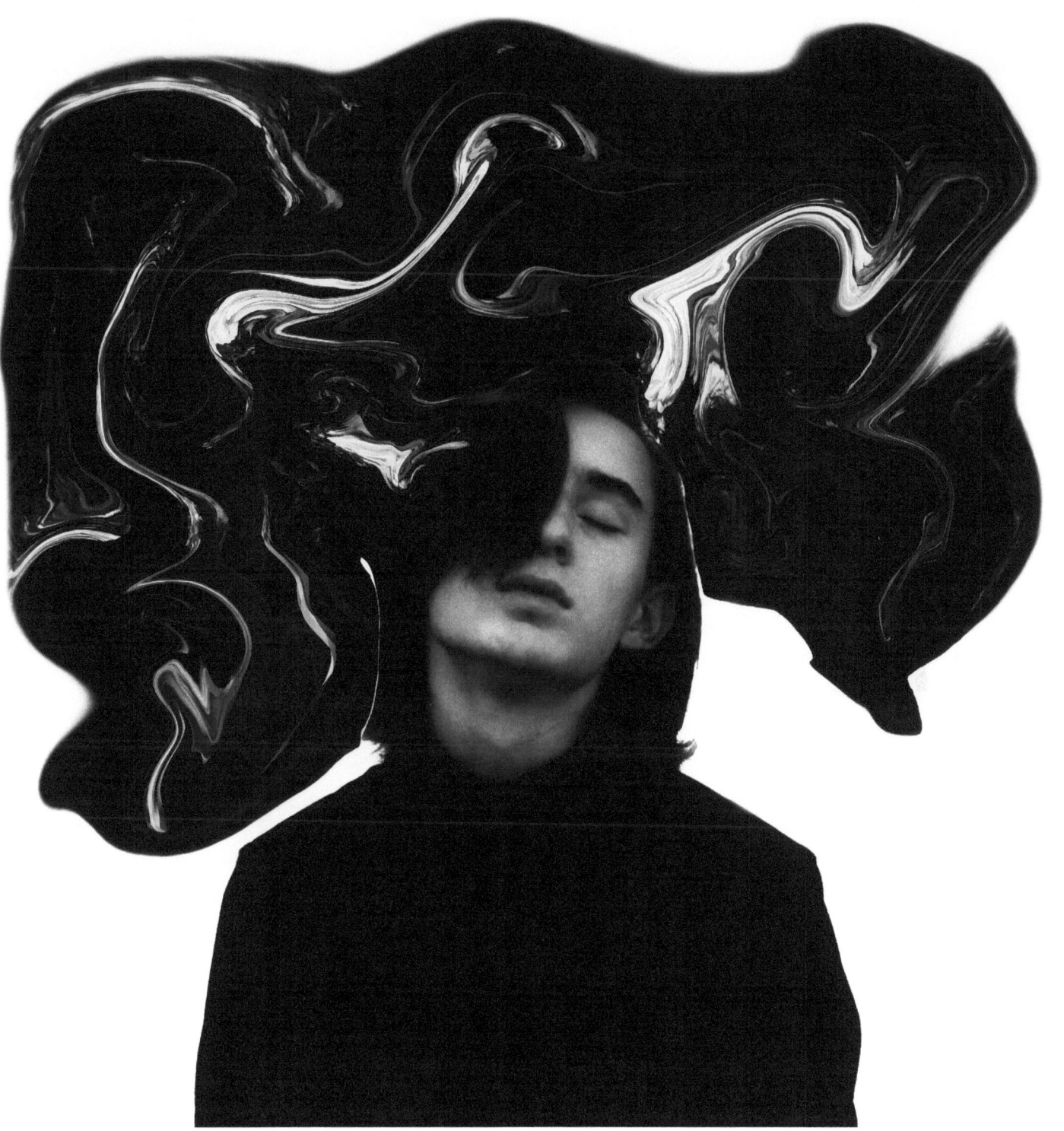

ALTERNATE ~~VERSIONS~~

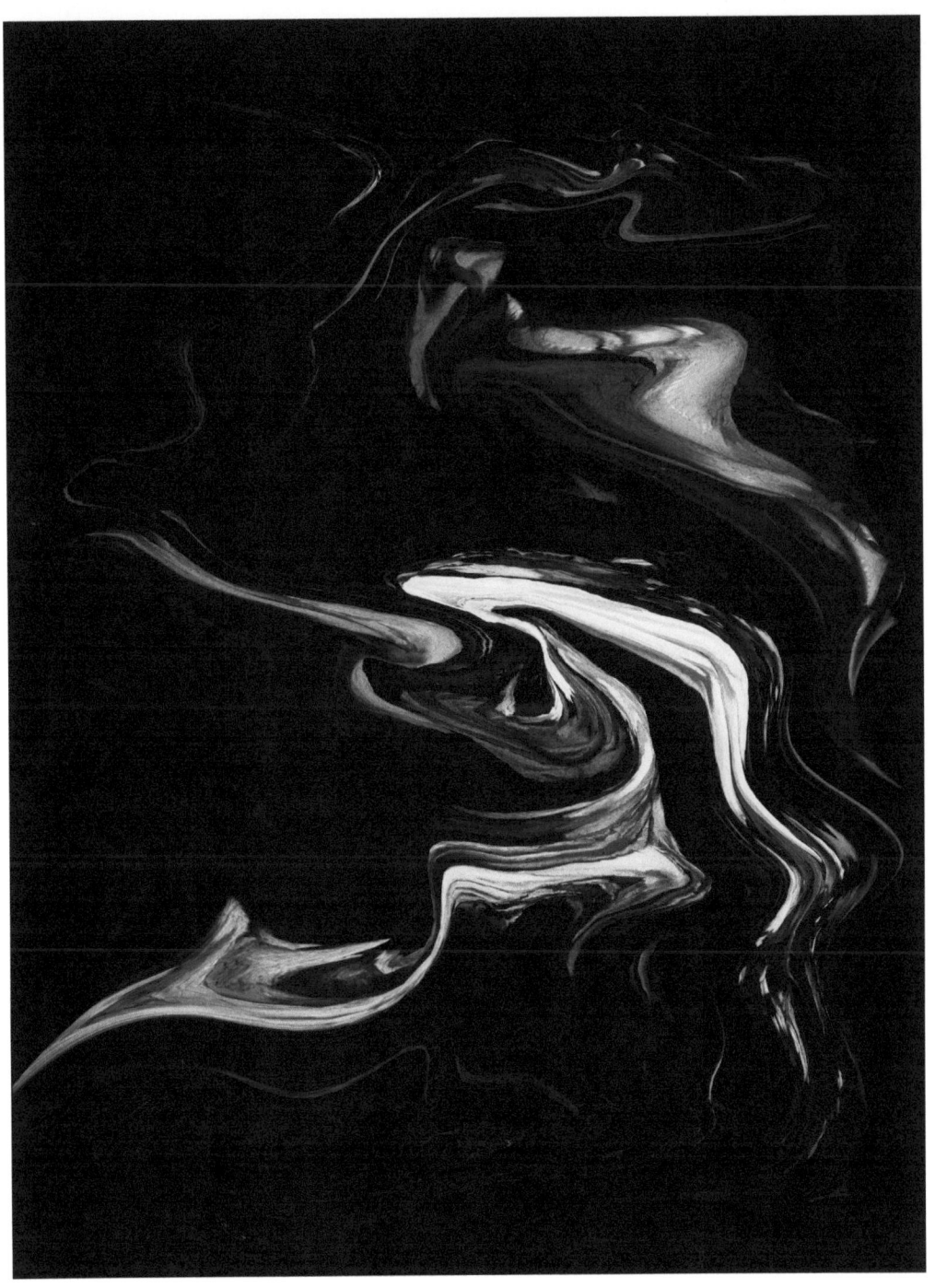

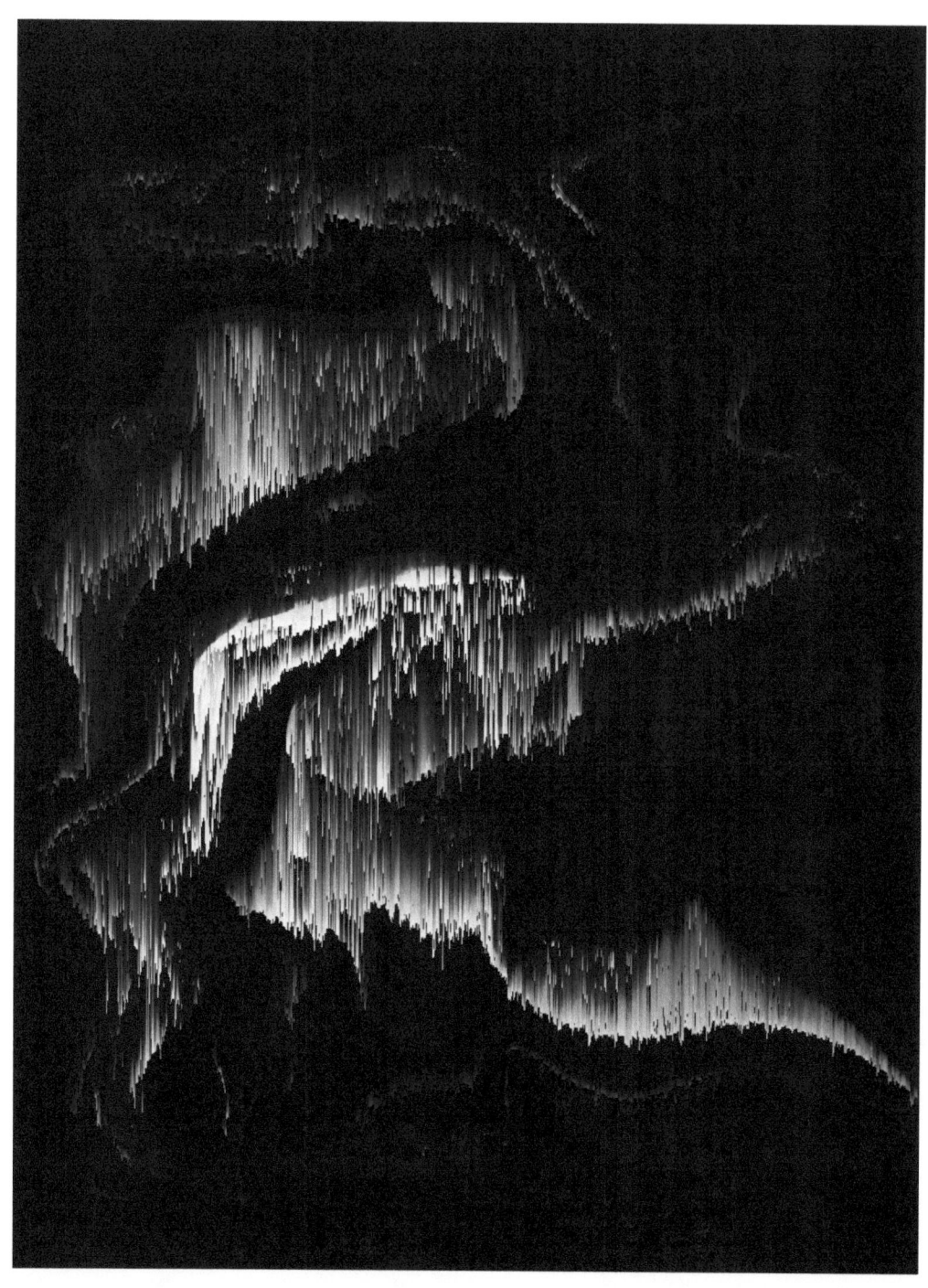

One of the aesthetics I chose for the album was more of a Digital Glitch look. You can spot the digital glitch style in music videos and ads for the album. However, the main look for the album was the natural abstract looking Oil on Canvas clashed with photography look. However, all the artwork had its place in the end.
All the artwork was experimental at the core.

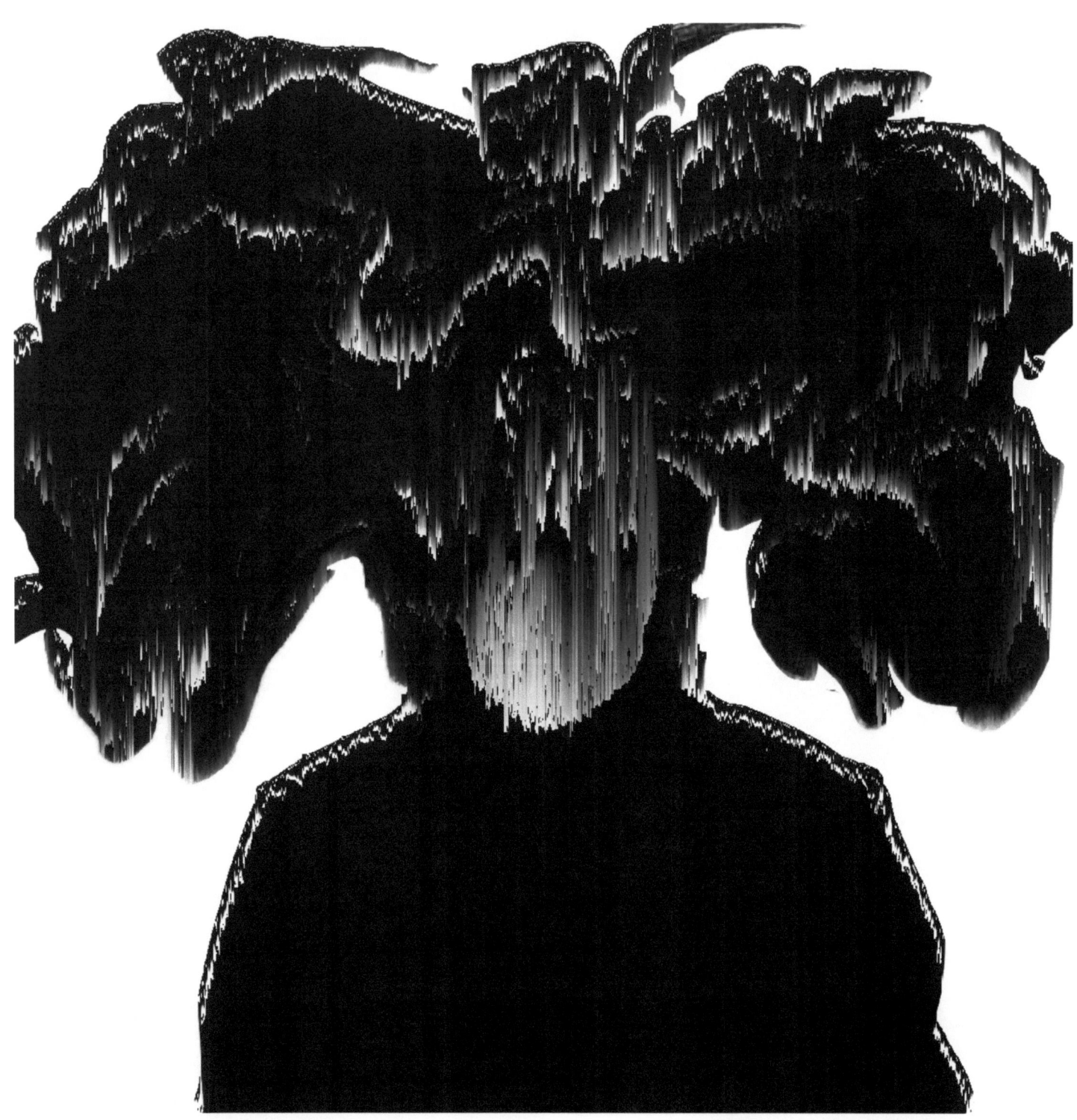

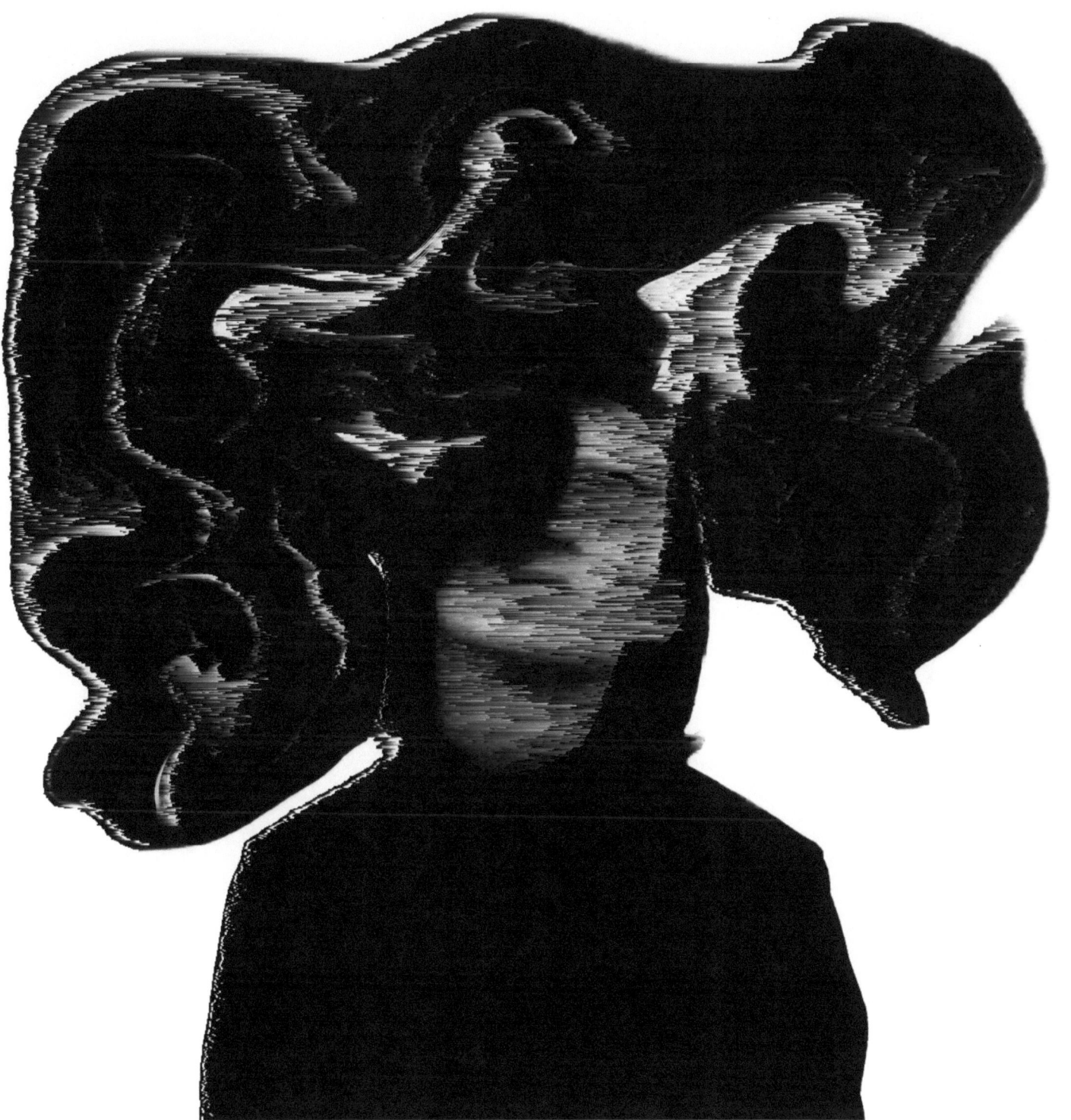

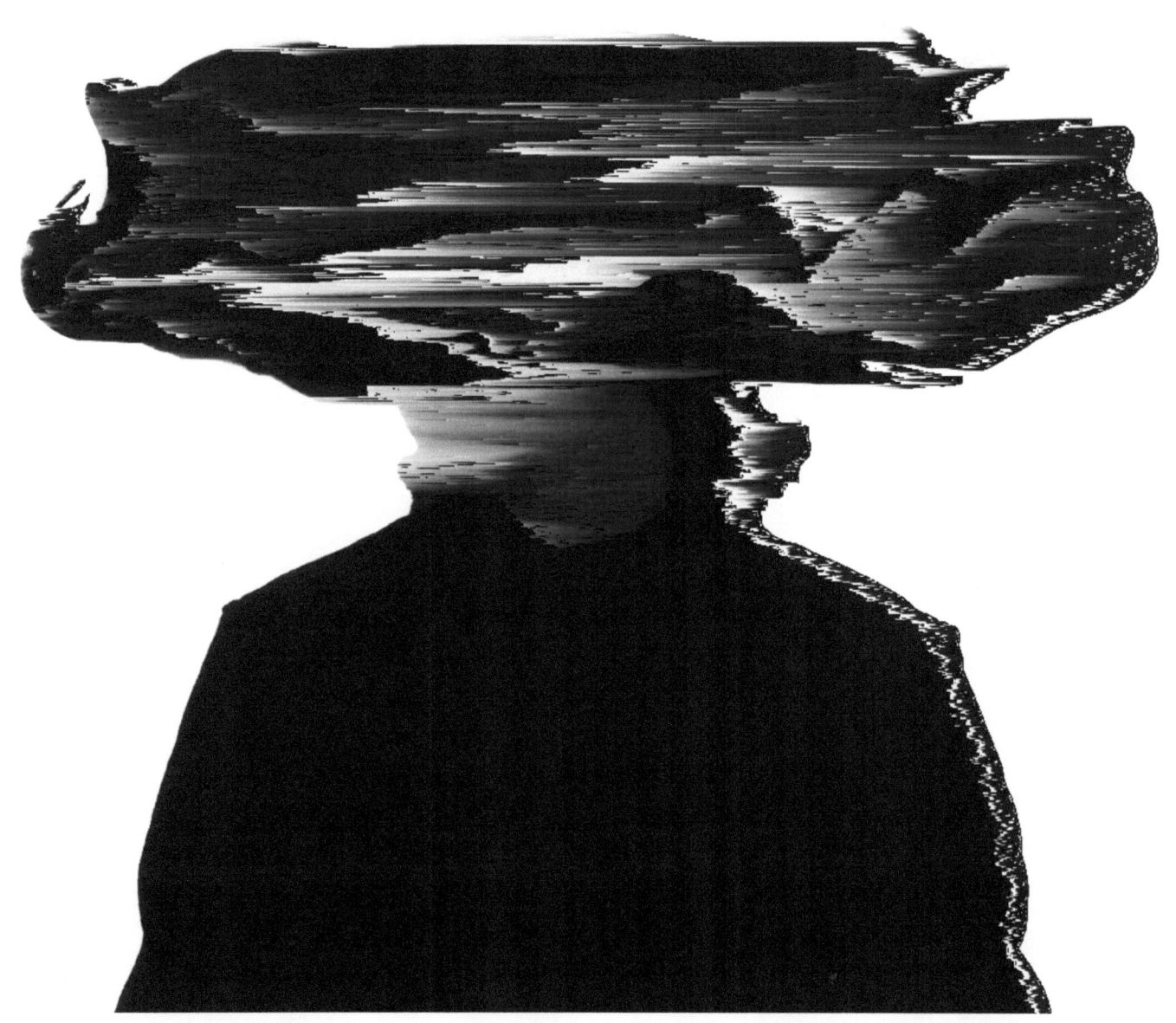

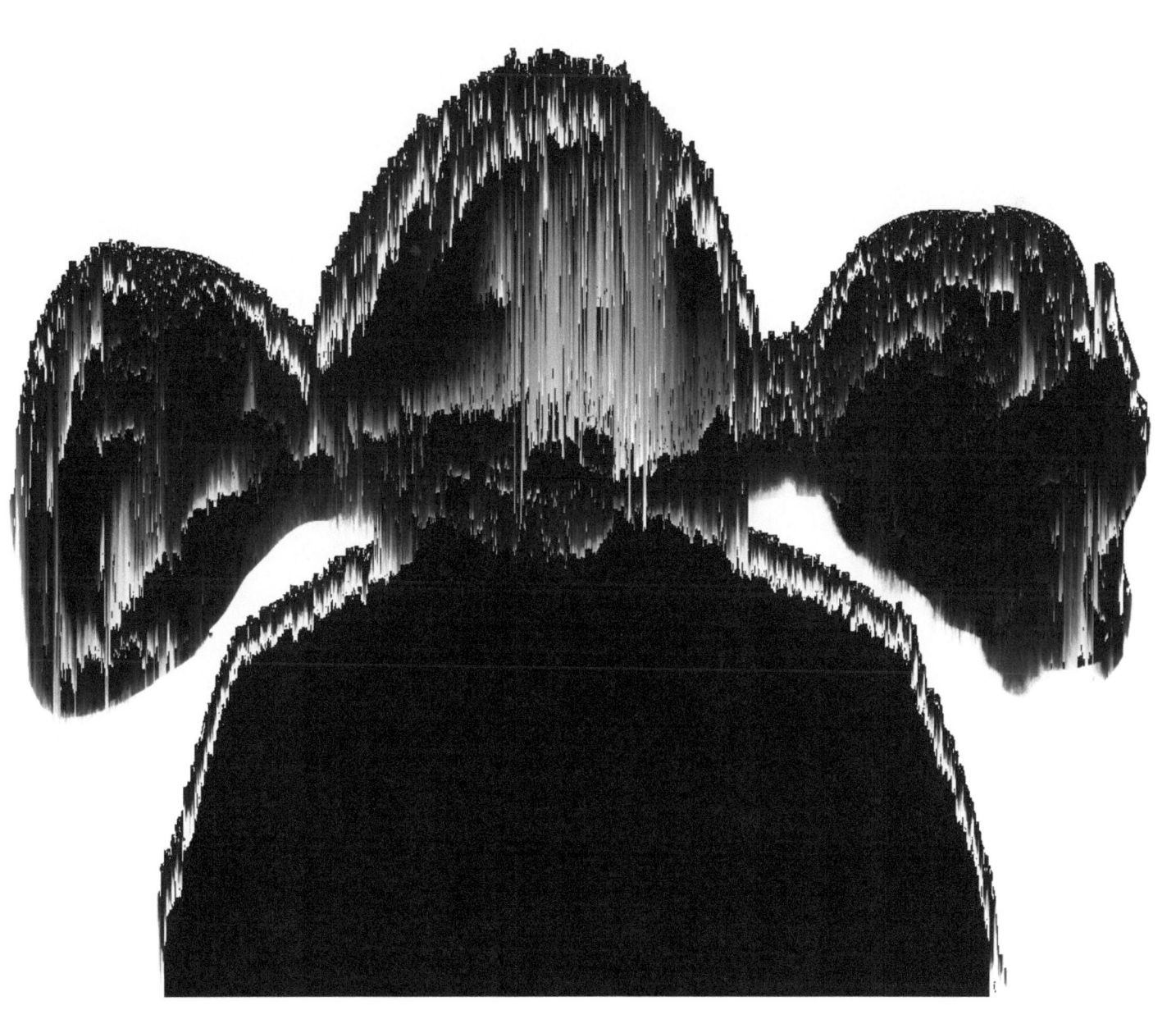

+ The *Polaroid* Edits +

~

There was a point in the design process where I created Polaroid Mockups; these designs were later released as limited edition stickers.

They did have a unique look, but ultimately I felt they would be lost in the whole 'nostalgic' polaroid trend. I didn't think they'd stand out enough. But I was very pleased with how many people loved the stickers.

Again, they are all alternate album covers.

~

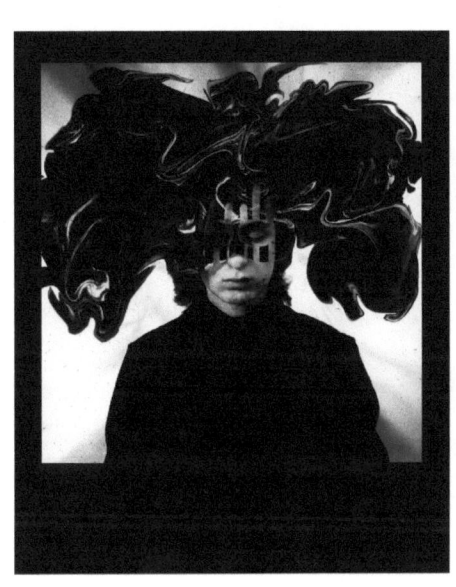 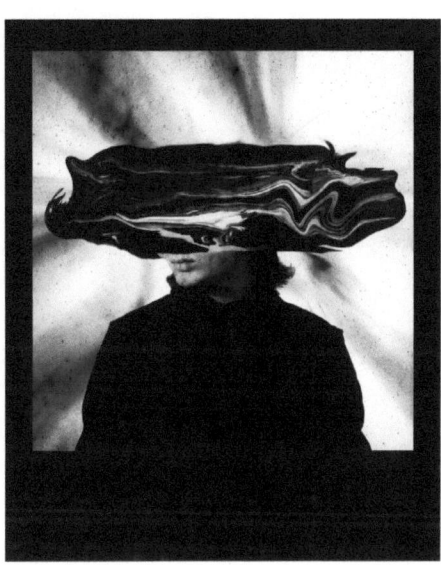 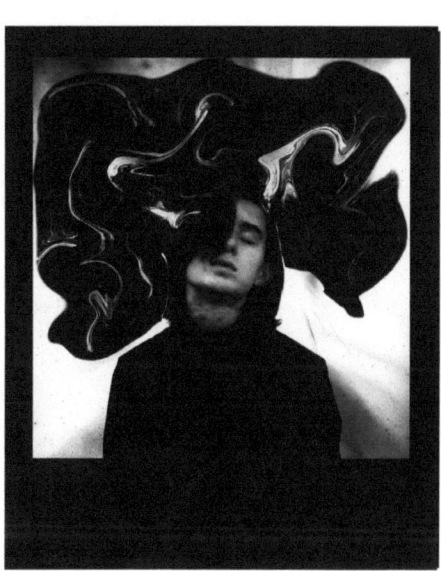

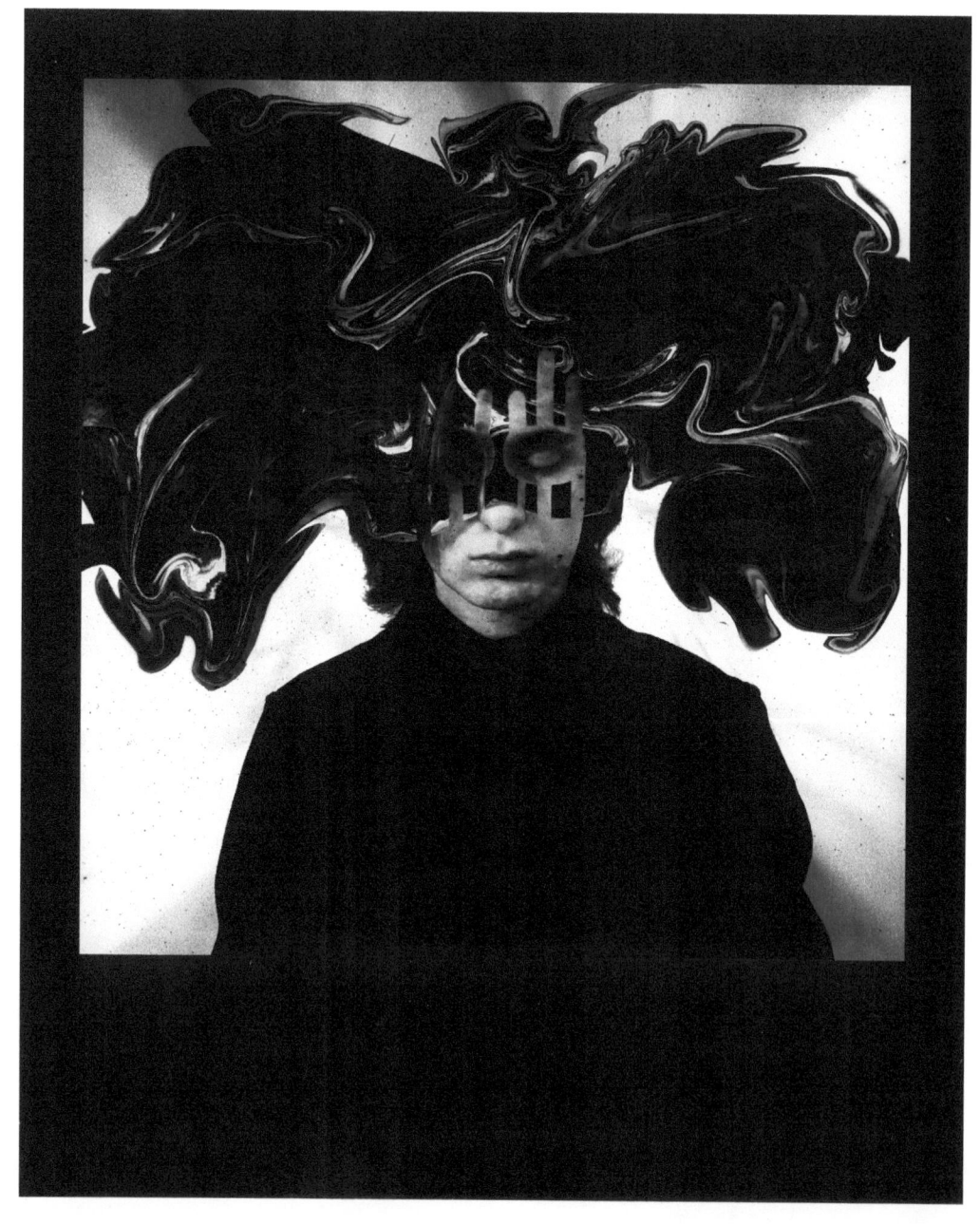

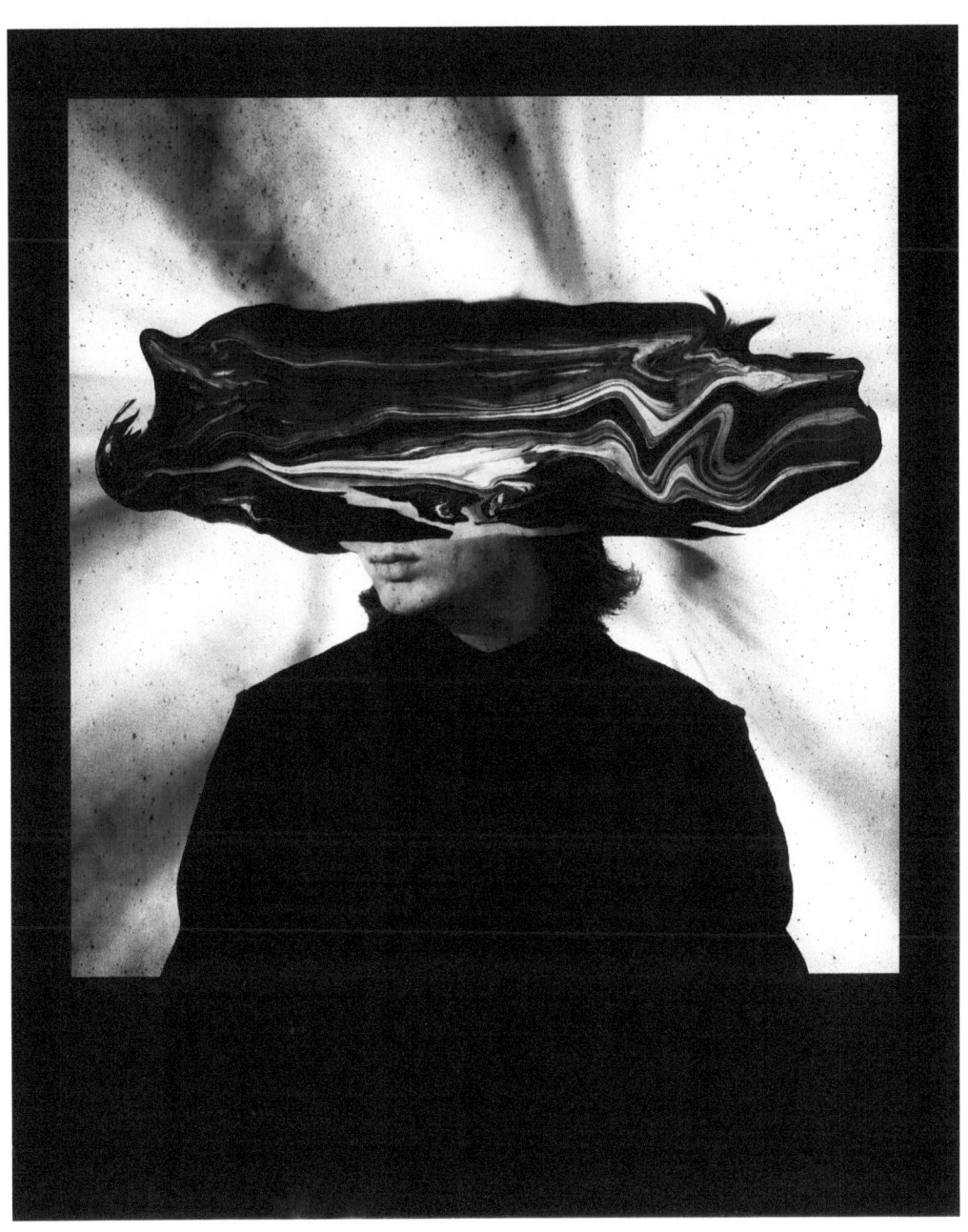

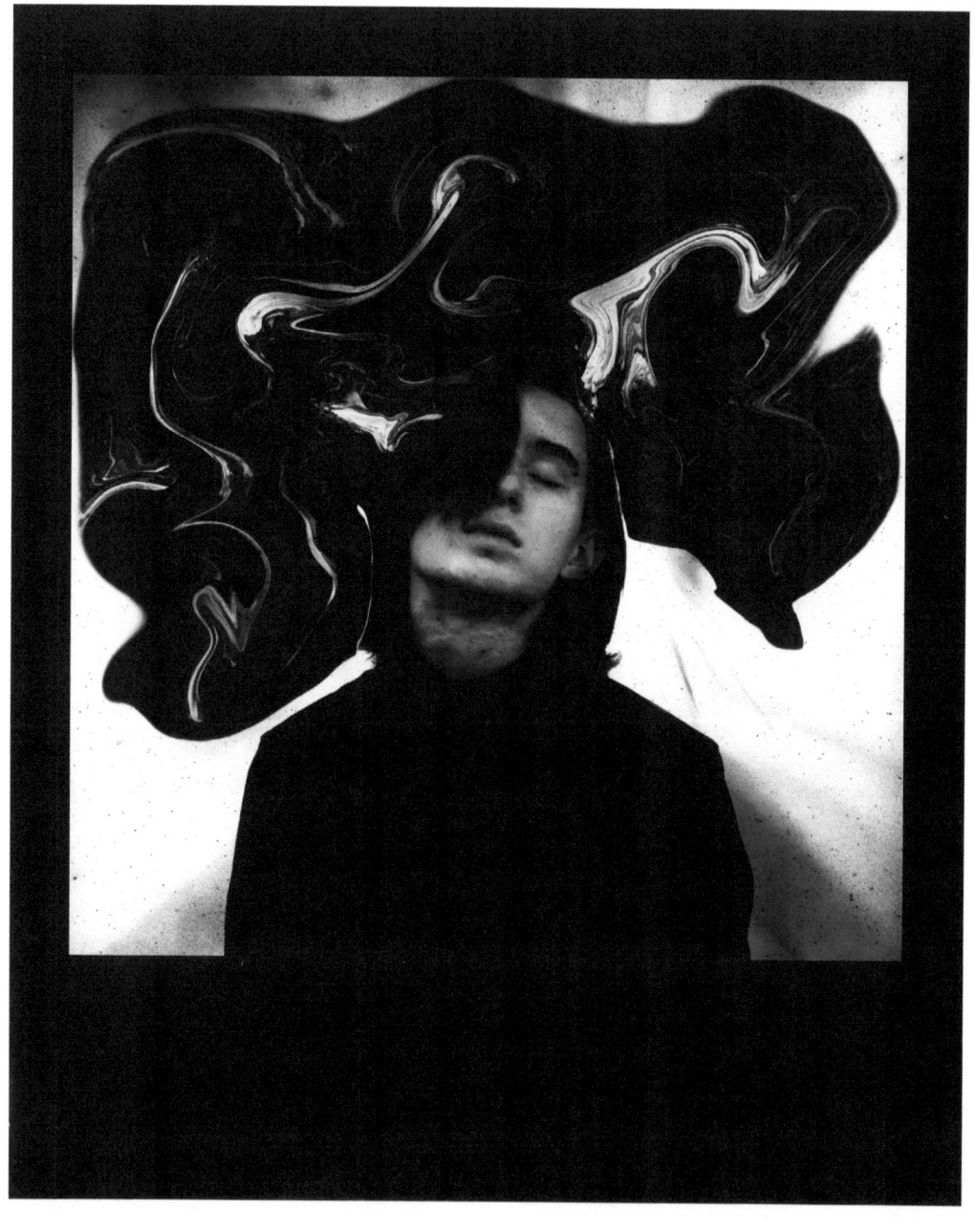

The reasoning behind why I didn't use these Polaroid Edits in the official album release is that I felt that they were to 'confined' to the shape of the polaroid film. They didn't have the look I was loving with the rest of the final album art.

But as usual, when creating a bunch of artwork for an album there is always outtakes. Not all the art can be shared, at the time of release. I wanted the artwork to be eye-catching, but still draw people to the music.

+ THE **INVERTED** VERSIONS +

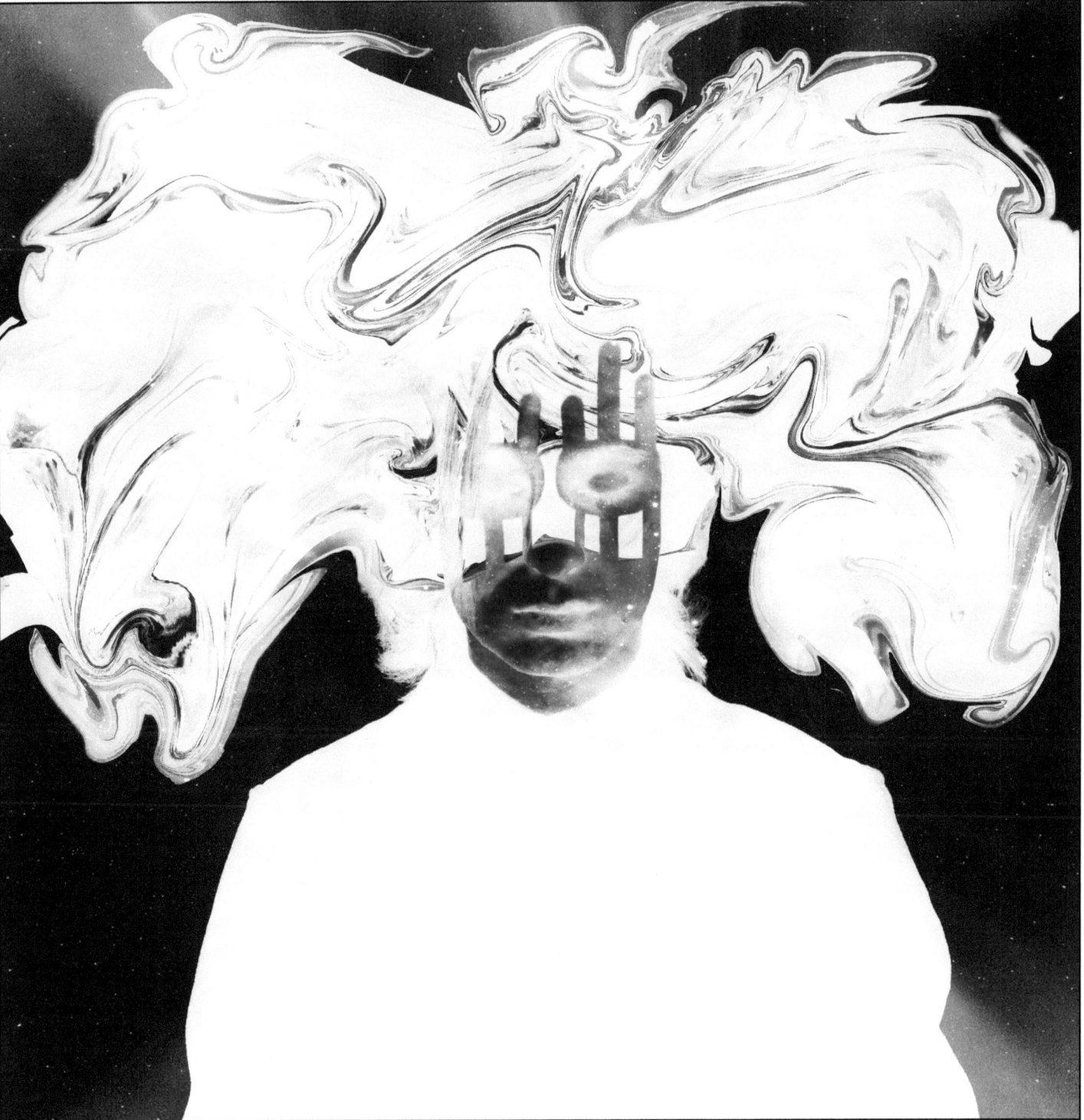

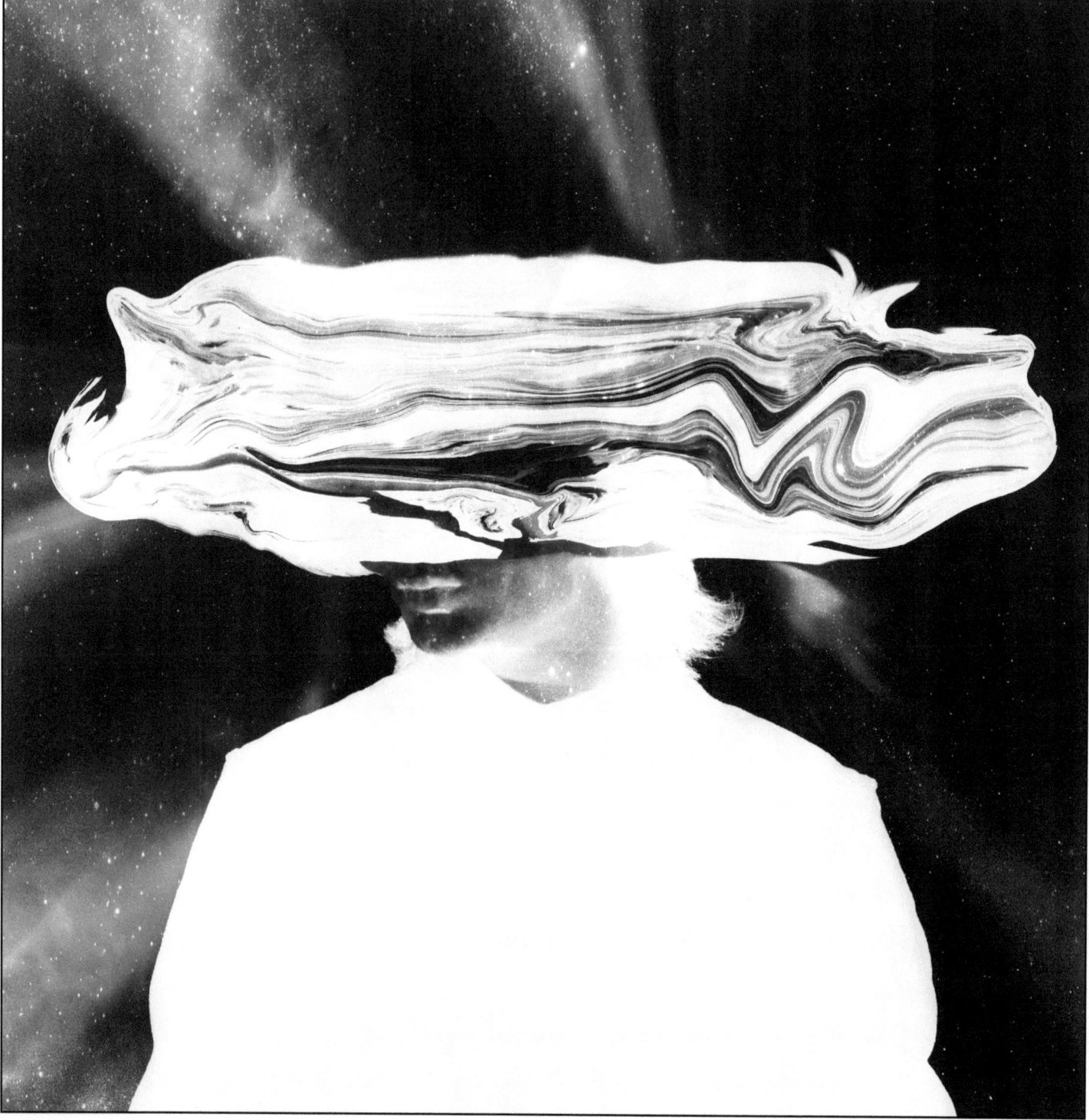

Through out making all the art pieces, I wanted to get a bit more experimental. I ran the images through an Inverted filter. Or "negative" filter. I loved how they looked but wanted to save them for a Deluxe version of the album - that never actually happened, unfortunately. Because I felt the album didn't need a re-release.

But they looked great and they had their own type of character, I suppose. However, just like all the art for this album, they were experimental at the core. But these images, I felt they didn't capture what I was looking for. Unlike the original counterparts.

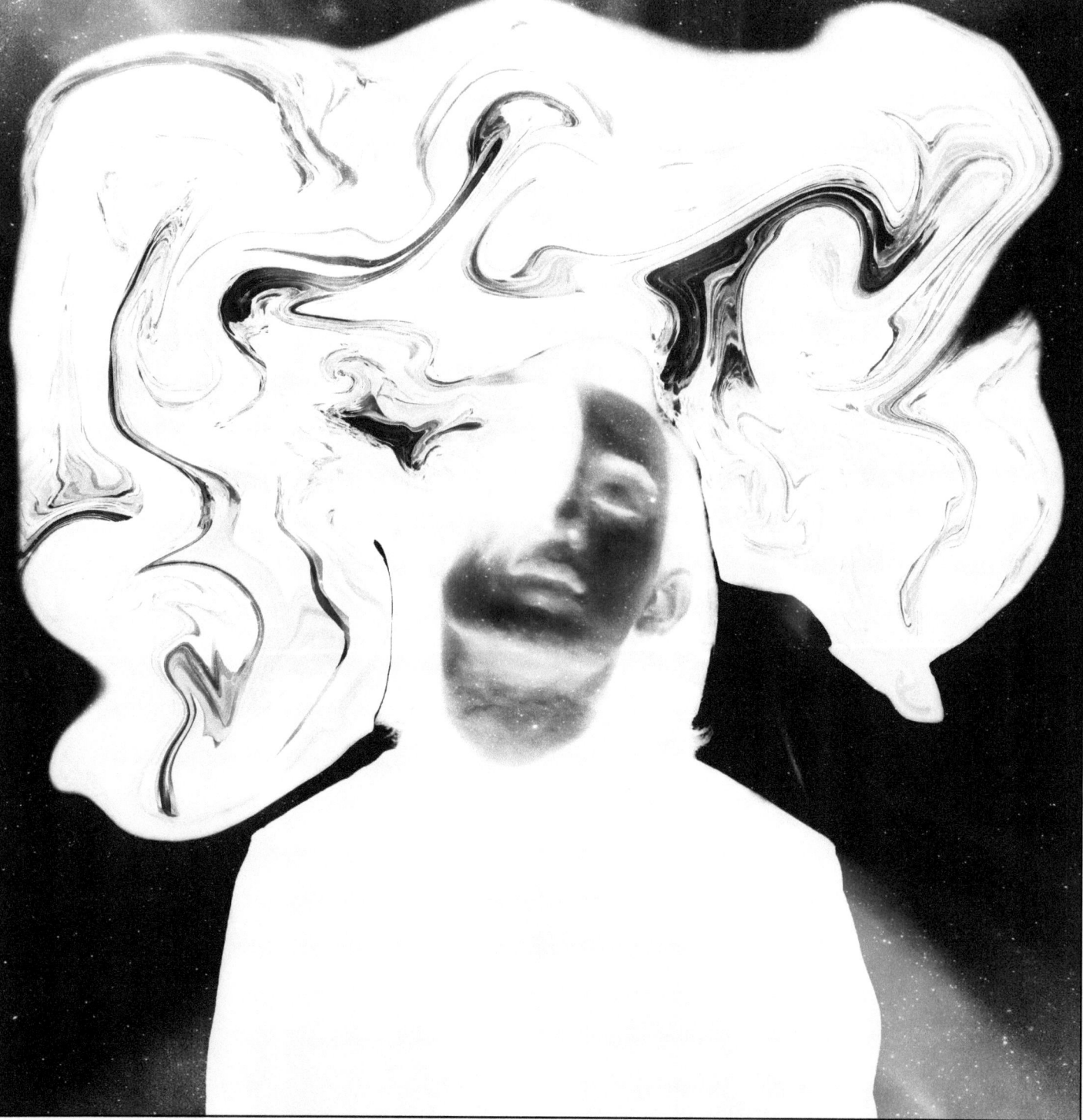

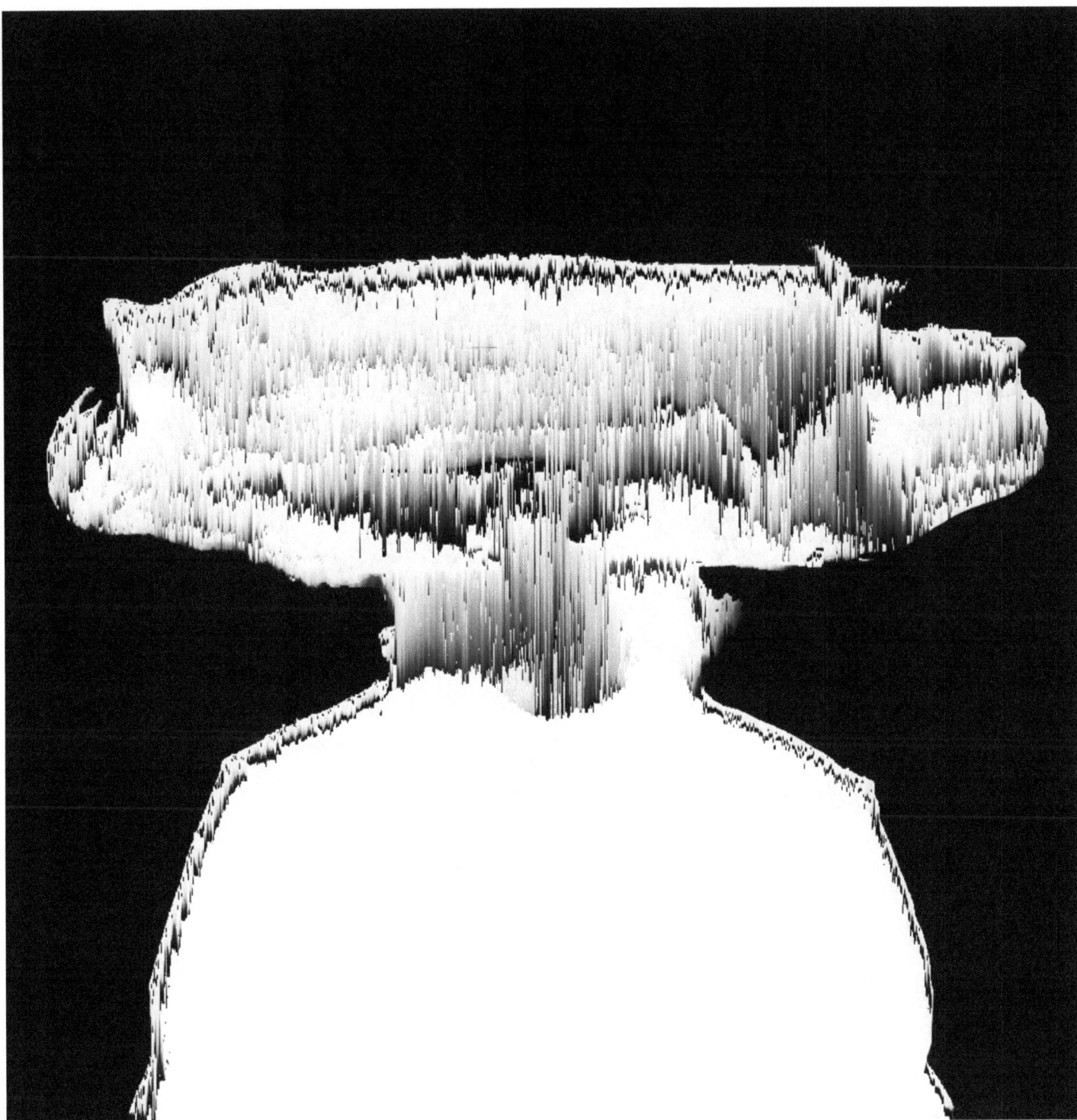

+ CONCLUSION +

In the beginning some did find my experimental artwork a bit on the dramatic side. And some even felt that none of the artwork even remotely suited the music style. But now that the album has been out since August 2020, the Love and Support for the album outweighs the critics by so much.

I don't think any of my past albums have had such a personal impact on me. And I don't think I've gotten so many personal messages from people who have listened to the music telling me about how the album helped them. This album was so different from my past albums. I've been told by many that the music has made them feel seen and understood in so many ways. And I am so unbelievably thankful that so many people loved the music and artwork.

I'm excited for what the future holds, and I am so blessed to call myself an Artist.

If I'm going to continue to create art, it might as well be as Odd, Strange, Bold, and even as Dramatic as I am.

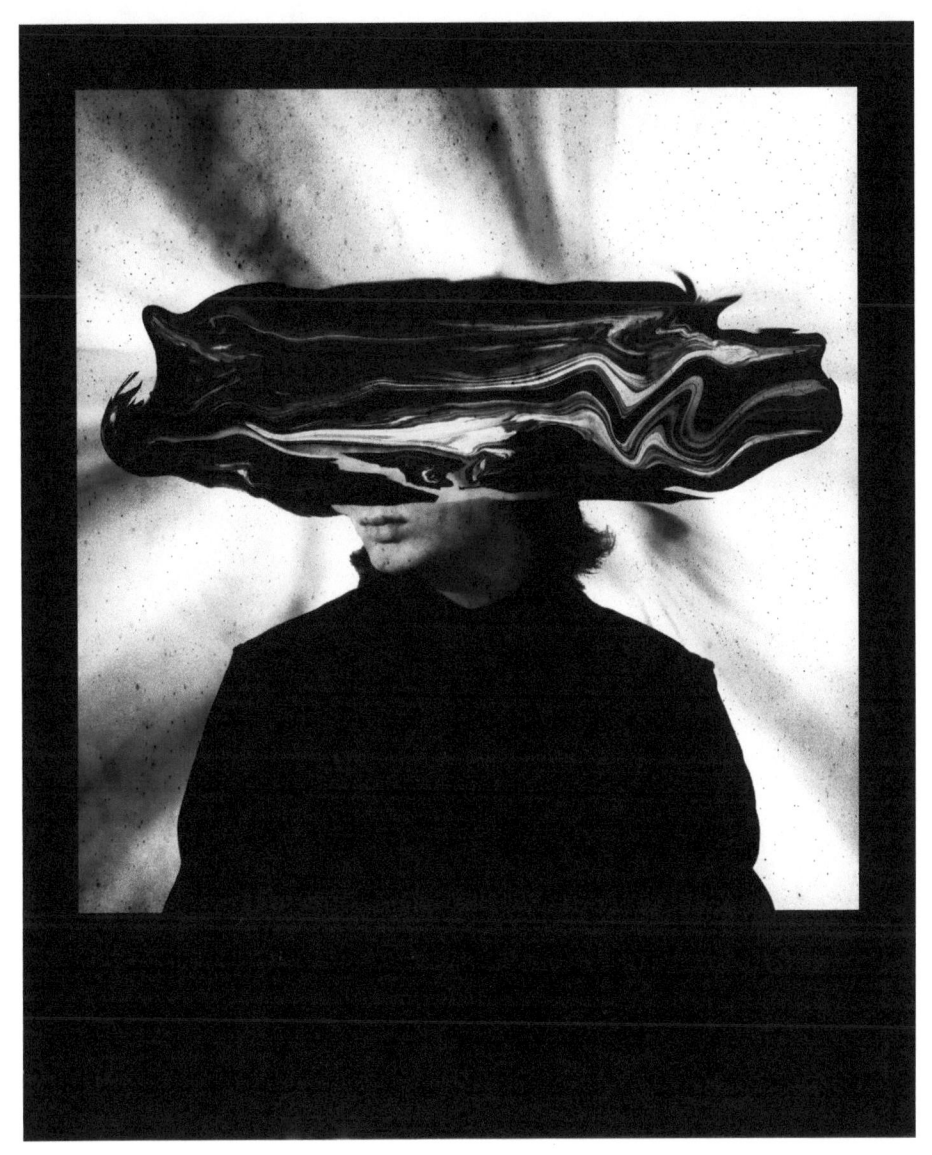

THE EARTH OPENED WIDE
+ S K Y L E R L O Y D +

Thank you for being a part of my journey.

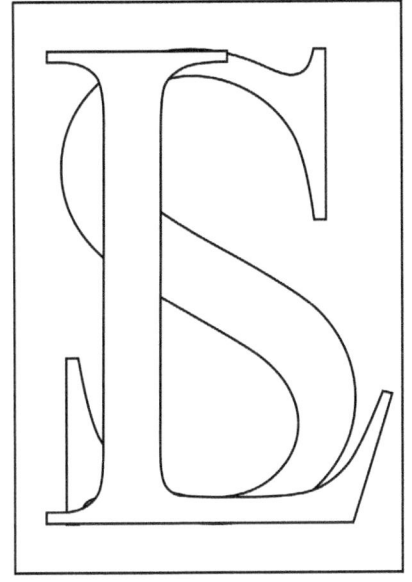

+ SKYLER LOYD +

SKYLER LOYD

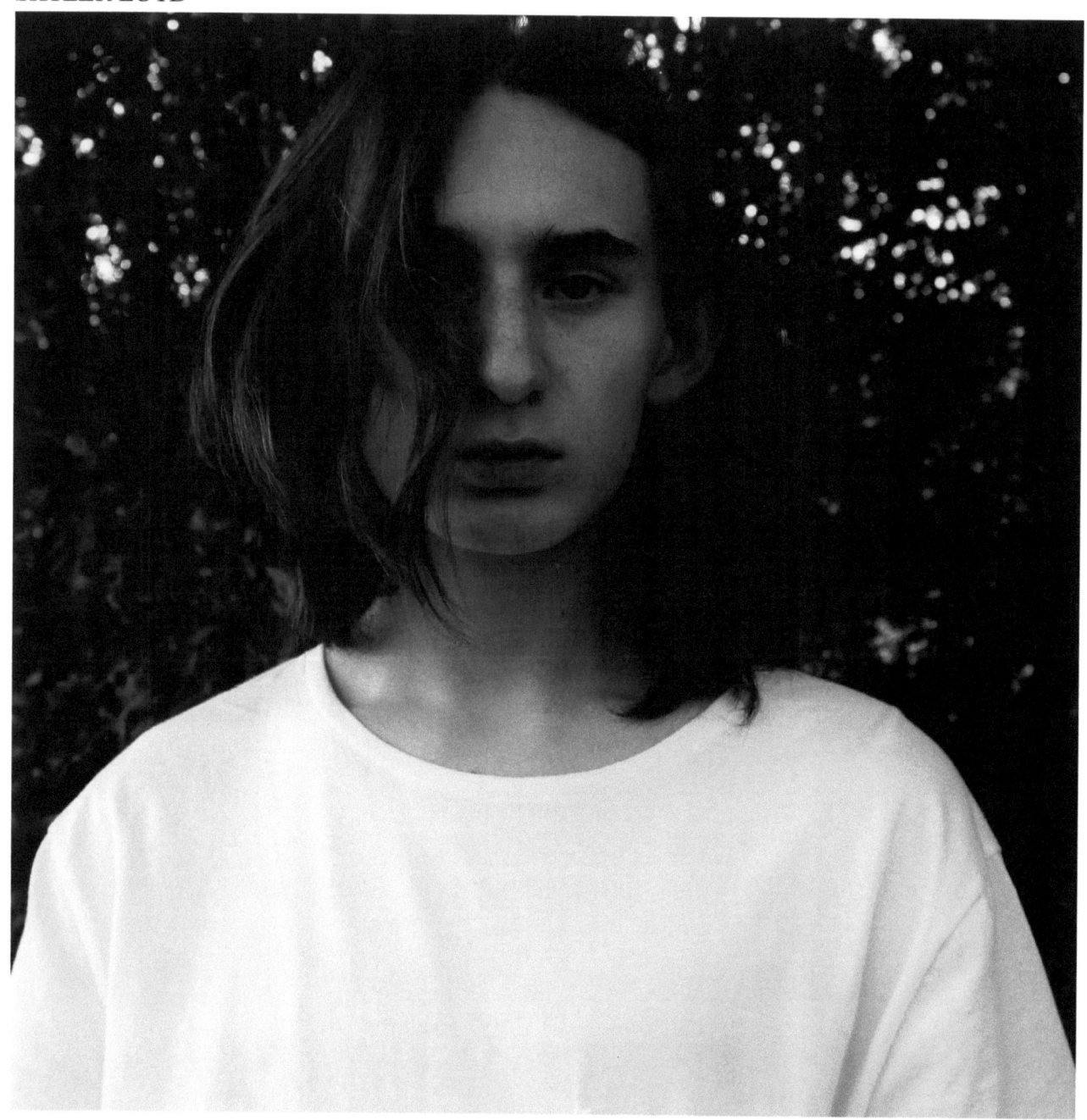

AUGUST 2020

+ ABOUT THE AUTHOR +

Skyler Loyd is a Neo-Classical / New Age Musician / Composer, Visual Artist and Writer primarily based out of Farmington, New Mexico. Loyd's music clashes with Experimental as well as Ambient soundscapes. Loyd's primary instrument is the Piano, but he grew up playing Violin and Cello.

+ ABOUT THE ALBUM +

"The Earth Opened Wide" is a deeply Cathartic and Emotional Album by Skyler Loyd. "The Earth Opened Wide" is a Dark New Age / Experimental Album. From the deep raw strings. The cries of the orchestra, Melancholic melodies and Experimental soundscapes "The Earth Opened Wide" is an Emotionally charged atmosphere. A journey from Lost, Broken and Hurt to Found, Freed and Healed. A true story told through music.

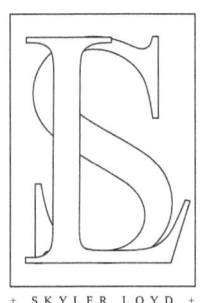

www.skylerloyd.com

Instagram / Facebook
@skylerloydofficial

© 2020-2022 SKYLER LOYD MUSIC ALL RIGHTS RESERVED

ALL WORKS ARE PROTECTED BY LAW

www.ingramcontent.com/pod-product-compliance
Lightning Source LLC
Chambersburg PA
CBHW040408220526
45473CB00004B/1169